COWBOYS

Catriona Clarke
Designed by Laura Parker
Illustrated by Terry McKenna

Cowboys consultant: Donald W. Reeves,
National Cowboy & Western Heritage Museum

Reading consultant: Alison Kelly,
Roehampton University

Contents

What is a cowboy?

Cowboys ride horses and look after cows. There have been cowboys all over the world for hundreds of years.

In Argentina, cowboys are called gauchos.

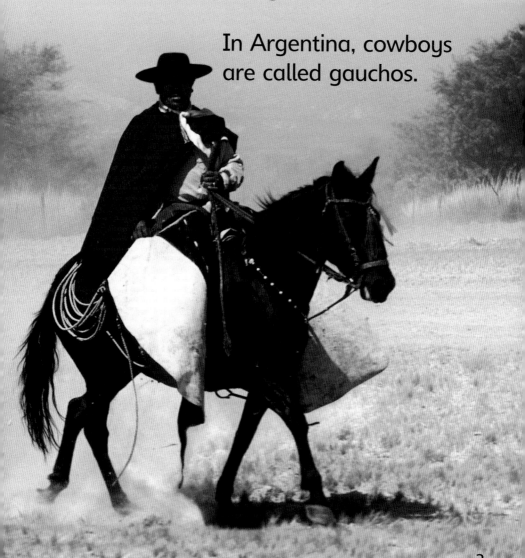

The Wild West

The most famous cowboys lived in the American West over 100 years ago.

Not many people lived in the West. There was lots of open space.

Most cowboys were young men - the work was too hard when they got older.

Cowboys liked riding horses and being outside in the fresh air.

They wanted jobs that had lots of freedom and fun...

... but they didn't get paid very much money for their work.

The open range

Cows were reared on farms called ranches. The ranches didn't have fences to keep the cows in, so they often wandered away.

A cowboy called a line rider had to ride around the edges of the ranch.

He herded cows back onto the ranch and made sure they were safe and well.

Lots of ranches had cows like these.
They are called Texas Longhorns.

The line rider also
guarded against
rustlers who tried
to steal cows.

He camped out by
himself every night.
It could be a very
lonely job.

What to wear

Cowboys wore comfortable clothes, but they liked to look good too.

They wore boots with heels so that their feet didn't slip out of their stirrups.

They wore chaps to protect their legs from sharp thorns and branches.

Lots of cowboys wore bandannas to keep the dust out of their faces.

Every cowboy wore a hat. The wide brim kept the sun and rain off the cowboy's face.

A cowboy could even use his hat to let his horse have a drink.

Cowboys hated walking, so it didn't matter if their boots were really uncomfortable.

Horsing around

A cowboy needed a good horse to help him do his job well.

Cowboys liked horses that were fast and steady on their feet, like this one.

Some cowboys spent so much time riding that they walked bow-legged.

A wild horse had to be broken in before a cowboy could ride it safely.

The cowboy lassoed the horse to catch it. Later, he could put a saddle on its back.

The cowboy twisted the horse's ear to distract it while he mounted it.

The horse kicked a few times. Then, it settled down and let the cowboy ride it.

11

Branding time

Every year, all the new calves had to be branded. A brand was a mark to show who owned each calf.

A cowboy separated one calf from the herd and lassoed it with a rope.

The calf was wrestled onto its side and the rope was untied.

Another cowboy branded the calf with a very hot branding iron.

Then, the calf was allowed to go back to the herd to find its mother.

Rustlers still stole cows, even though the cows had been branded.

The rustlers in this painting have been spotted by some cowboys in the distance.

Some rustlers wore horseshoes on the bottom of their shoes so their footprints couldn't be tracked.

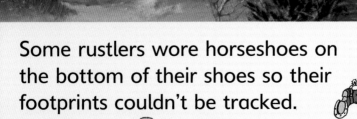

On the trail

When cows were old enough to be killed for their meat, they were taken on a long journey. This was called a trail drive.

A trail drive could last for months. It was hard work for the cowboys.

Food was cooked on a chuck wagon. Cowboys often ate biscuits and beans.

In the evening, some cowboys liked to tell stories and sing songs.

Cowboys liked to play jokes on each other - like putting a frog in someone's hat!

At night, cowboys took turns to keep watch for rustlers and wild animals.

At the end of the trail, the cows were taken by train to be sold in towns.

15

Danger!

Life on the cattle trail was often very dangerous for cowboys.

A cowboy could die of thirst if he couldn't find water to drink.

The cowboy in this painting has found some water in a hollow in the desert.

Sometimes cows got scared by a loud noise, like thunder.

They started to snort and wander around in circles.

If one cow broke away from the herd, it caused a stampede.

The cows ran wild, trampling everything in their path.

Cowboys had to check their boots for snakes and scorpions before they put them on.

Going to town

After a long time on the cattle trail, cowboys looked forward to going to town.

A cowboy washed in a river for the first time in months.

He went into the town for a shave and a haircut.

He bought new clothes to replace his old, tattered ones.

Then, he went to a saloon to eat, drink and have fun.

After just a few days in town, cowboys had often spent all the money they'd earned.

Some cowboys caused trouble in the towns they visited.

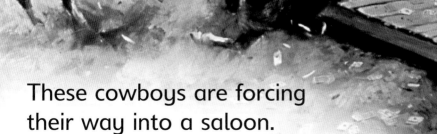

These cowboys are forcing their way into a saloon.

Sharpshooting

A sheriff's job was to protect a town and make sure cowboys didn't cause trouble.

Sheriffs were often very good at shooting. They were sometimes called 'gunslingers'.

The sheriff made sure that his guns were always clean and ready to use.

He wore his gun on a holster attached to his belt, so it was easy to reach.

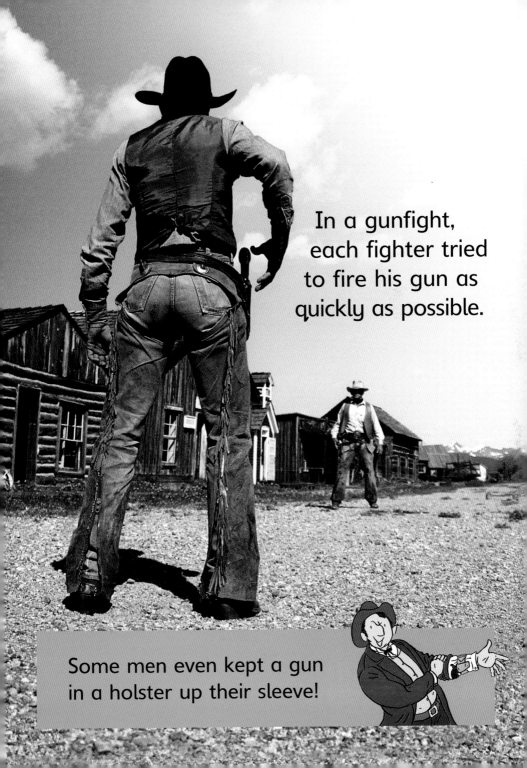

In a gunfight,
each fighter tried
to fire his gun as
quickly as possible.

Some men even kept a gun
in a holster up their sleeve!

Famous folk

Some people who lived in the Wild West became famous for different reasons.

Calamity Jane wore men's clothes and was very good at shooting.

Buffalo Bill ran a Wild West Show that went all over the world.

Wyatt Earp was in a very famous gunfight in a town called Tombstone.

This is a photograph
of Billy the Kid, the
most famous outlaw
in the West.

He was a cattle
rustler, and he killed
lots of people.

He was shot and
killed when he was
about 20 years old.

End of the road

By the end of the nineteenth century, the days of the Wild West were over.

Thousands of people arrived in the West. They built lots and lots of big farms...

... with barbed wire around them. Cows then couldn't roam on the open range.

A long railroad was built. It stretched across the whole country...

... so there was no need for cowboys to go on long trail drives any more.

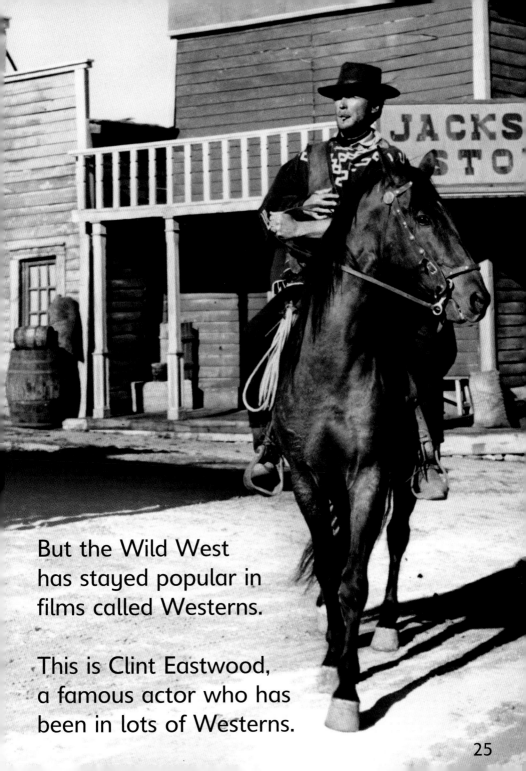

But the Wild West
has stayed popular in
films called Westerns.

This is Clint Eastwood,
a famous actor who has
been in lots of Westerns.

Rodeo riding

A rodeo is a competition of cowboy skills. Rodeos are still popular in America today.

In one event, a cowboy has to lasso a calf...

... and tie three of its legs together as quickly as he can.

In another event, a cowboy jumps off his horse...

... and wrestles one of the cattle down to the ground by its horns.

The most dangerous event is bull riding.

The bull bucks and kicks to try to get the cowboy off its back.

Rodeo cowboys never put their hats down on a bed - they think it's really bad luck!

Cowboys today

There are still cowboys around today. They wear the same clothes, but lots of other things have changed.

Some modern ranches look like this one.

The rancher grows crops to feed the cows and horses.

As well as horses, cowboys use trucks and trailers to get around...

... and sometimes even helicopters.

Tourists sometimes stay on a ranch to try being a cowboy for a while.

Glossary of cowboy words

Here are some of the words in this book you might not know. This page tells you what they mean.

 ranch - a large farm for rearing cows.

 stirrups - loops attached to the saddle. The cowboys' feet go in them.

 lasso - a rope with a loop at the end. The loop can be tightened.

 branding - marking cattle with a sign to show who owns them.

 trail drive - a journey that cattle go on from the ranch to the railroad.

 chuck wagon - a cooking and supply wagon used on a trail drive.

 outlaw - someone who has broken the law, but has not been caught.

Websites to visit

If you have a computer, you can find out more about cowboys on the Internet. On the Usborne Quicklinks Website there are links to four fun websites.

Website 1 - Dress a cowboy ready for the trail.

Website 2 - Listen to some cowboy songs.

Website 3 - Take a closer look at what's in a chuck wagon.

Website 4 - Try a cowboy wordsearch.

To visit these websites, go to **www.usborne-quicklinks.com** Read the Internet safety guidelines, and then type the keywords "beginners cowboys".

The websites are regularly reviewed and the links in Usborne Quicklinks are updated. However, Usborne Publishing is not responsible, and does not accept liability, for the content or availability of any website other than its own. We recommend that children are supervised while on the Internet.

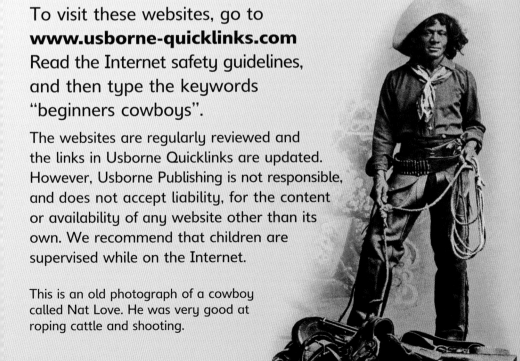

This is an old photograph of a cowboy called Nat Love. He was very good at roping cattle and shooting.

Index

Acknowledgements

Photographic manipulation by John Russell.

Photo credits

The publishers are grateful to the following for permission to reproduce material:
© **CORBIS** 1 (David Stoecklein), 4 (Christie's Images), 6-7 (David Stoecklein), 10 (Buddy Mays), 13 (Christie's Images), 23 (Bettmann), 25 (Bettmann) 27 (Bohemian Nomad Picturemakers), 31 (Bettmann); © **Private Collection/Peter Newark Western Americana/The Bridgeman Art Library** cover ('Texas Cowboy' by Stanley L. Wood {1866-1928}), 9 ('The Last Drop from his Stetson' American School), 16 ('The Water Hole' by Stanley L. Wood {1866-1928}), 19 ('In Without Knocking' by Charles Marion Russell {1865-1926}); **PunchStock/Comstock** 21; © **Westend61/Alamy** 2-3.

Vikings

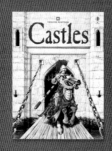
Castles

How flowers grow

Knights

Living in space

Caterpillars and Butterflies

Ballet

Pirates

Egyptians

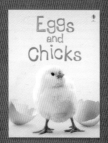
Eggs and Chicks

Romans

Dinosaurs

Tadpoles and frogs

Why do we eat?

Under the sea

Weather

Sun, Moon and Stars

Farm animals

Elizabeth I

RUBBISH AND RECYCLING